SOMETHING LIKE BONES

HANNAH DONOVAN

ISBN 978-81-19654-07-9

Published 2024 by Cyberwit.net
HIG 45 Kaushambi Kunj, Kalindipuram
Allahabad - 211011 (U.P.) India
http://www.cyberwit.net
E-mail: info@cyberwit.net

Book and cover design by Hannah Donovan
Cover art by Hannah Donovan
www.hannahdonovanart.com

CONTENTS

SOMETHING LIKE BONES

Something like bones ache.
I say *something like bones* because

I am neither scientist
nor spiritualist, or rather

I am both, but not yet poet enough
to possess the language

to describe your flight,
and the settling without.

I can say: It is more human
and also less, this sensation.

I can say: Something
like bones ache.

BEFORE

NORTH STAR

You said the floor was lava and I believed it,
steadied myself on a doorknob,
perched on tiptoes, a meek attempt
at ascension from old wood.

You recalled a face on the ceiling,
a many-armed being, a warmth
my body could not provide and I
clung to the webbing between your words
to fill the pit of mystery you clanged around in,
fingering blindly for the discovery of your substance.
          (lava: no)
          (hollow: maybe)

You scolded my morning tongue
for sleepily relaying a sour dream
and I checked my mouth for wasps
in the bathroom mirror while
you kept the covers stirring,
your own thoughts buzzing sweet.

You told me of my conundrum:
a leaf-cutter ant, self-aware, hauling
a load it knows not what for, swallowed
by a Sisyphean fate in some remote jungle,
the nights too dark for stars, and so
I fastened my weight to your hind legs,
our pace slowing to a crawl,
my inner compass running haywire,
my psyche weakening at the knees,
squinting eyes through canopies
to glimpse Mecca, closing eyes

to trust your North, my echo
sounding in your every chamber,
throat swelling shut with sting welts.

You warned me of your nature:
volatile as wave on lava rock,
stubborn as Sisyphus, hauling.
I believed it. I had seen it.

I buckled down, tightened the knots,
smashed the inner compass running haywire.
Eyes welded skyward, skyward searching,
searching for the glint, the hint of a glimmer,
perhaps dimly burning, perhaps never born,
in a sky too dark, too dark for stars.

LET

Man likes to tell the salmon
how to be better fish.
Let us build you nets!
Let us harvest your eggs!
Let us push artificial jet streams into your faces!
(for you – of course – have forgotten how to go upstream)

I wish you'd stop telling me
how to be a better lover.
My body knows falling water,
upriver desire, the direction
of home.

My hopes sink for Man,
for Men,
for Future.

A statistic floats:
Populations double when
we do nothing with our hands
and ideas.
Let the Coho bounce back!
Let my heart be, it knows the rhythm of swim.

CYCLE

i sit
drip blood
think i am
such a giver
(whether
i want to be
or not)
where's your effort
your trail of crumbs
leading to
better understanding
safer sex
i love you
you matter
come here
i am spinning out
a busted dryer
cycling on low
puffing hot air
from lungs
waiting to be
filled with song
tell me when to stop
i do not know when
surrender is not
my strong suit
draw a line
in the sand
or anywhere
soft but definite
so i can see
oh this needs to
this needs to end.

THE RING

"One more punch,"
Says the bloody fighter,
"I have it in me."

Raising a slack arm
To collapse in just
The right place, he
Sputters: "This will be
The one to win it."

He eggs his opponent on:
"Come. Closer," eyes
Bleary from sweat
And swollen over.

He swings and catches dead air.
Again he paws and misses.
Again. Again.

He lifts the sick weight of his head.
All the spectators have gone home.
The announcer has left the mic
Swinging from its ceiling cord.
He is the only one in the ring.

Gloved hands wobbling, he stays down.
Gums throbbing, he stays down.
Limbs spent, he stays down.
Will bent, he stays down.

TIPPING POINT

a found poem

We were right in the thick of it.
            at each other's throats.

Where things get murky is in the
trappings.
            a dark room can look and feel
            freely available to perform

a similar pattern spares a thought for the sad

The disappearing act became a
            surrealistic faith in accidents,

the chemical madness, holding on
            for dear life to the frame
cannot pretend that reality is manipulable

            I think a tipping point has been reached.

[Image of original collage work on pgs. 58 and 59]

I'M LEAVING

I'm leaving
You heard me right
I'm leaving
I'm finally fed up
With your nonsense
And you can't stop me

I'm about to leave I just need to find my jacket and
Gather my toothbrush and fold some of your socks
The way you like and then I. Am. Gone.
You'll never hear from me again

What's that?
Yes, I *have* put the kettle on
I'm hoarse from yelling and I need
A spot of tea to calm my frazzled nerves –
Lord knows you won't drink the chamomile
After I turn tail and go

You're a shit person
You don't care about me one bit
And I am sick of it
When you think of some retaliation
You can find me in the bath

Oh that's rich...you don't even beg!
You don't even say you're sorry
For all of your wrongdoing!
THIS – this is why I am leaving you
Hand me that extra blanket, will you?
And flip the lights off while you're up?
Thanks...I love you too...Good night

GANNY

ga•nny [gan-ee] *n.* a slang term for a Narragansett (beer).

He called it a Ganny.
My West Coast ass never heard that
so I laughed.
It was funny, after all.
He was funny. I wasn't.
That was our deal. Apparently.

"Another round?"
Another round.

I confessed I was nervous about
my heart murmur. Doctor just found it.
He rolled his eyes and sighed:
Here we go again, with the negativity.

"Another round?"

Another round.

On birthdays,
he always said
he'd had the idea to
get me this or that but then...didn't.
Happy Birthday!

"Another round?"

Another round.

At the Kevin Morby concert he told me
I needed to be more *emotionally mature.*
He ditched me on the way home:
biked away from an adult conversation
at 30 miles an hour.

"Another round?"

Another round.

He didn't collect me at Arrivals;
his car was in *a good spot.*
The next day he up and blazed
a thousand miles to bum-fuck Minnesota
for the weekend. He felt like it.

"Another round?"

Another round.

Over the phone he'd...wait, what am I saying?
He never wanted to talk on the phone.

"Another round?"

Another round.

I was invisible at his friend's wedding,
the one where he flirted with the bridesmaid.
When I went to sit in the car for
a quiet moment, I made *things look bad*
between us.

"Another round?"

Another round.

Our anniversary picnic: thwarted.
He wanted to go to the bar instead.
He invited his buddy along for the night.
We drank Gannies. I third wheeled.

"Another round?"

On the walk back, I mentioned the beer:
I had been disappointed by the taste,
wished I'd had something different.
You have to stop living a life of regret.
Then silence. Then his place.

"Another round?"

"Another round?"

I didn't follow him in.

ACHE

THE WALK
POST-CHAKRA CLEANSING

my energy worker told me
i shouldn't beg

but who's to say that's what it'll be?

sawdust and car exhaust
smell a lot like palo santo if you're in the right mind
and i am
swamped
in old memories
looking for a new miracle
so i take a big gulp of air
as i step over the transmission hose on grand
at morgan

the night wind gnaws at my wrists
and i'm wishing i'd grabbed the mittens
your mom bought me last christmas
before leaving the house

wound through a vintage shop
to pick out a piece i'll never take off for you
but the speaker blared through my calm and i left
empty handed

HOME:
RAMBLINGS FROM 11/17/18

floating past the waif with the heavy eyelids
and the ready-to-buy impatience of a chill millennial
        wrangler jeans in tow

every poem is an arm out to you.

        before i even realize who i'm addressing
        there it is:
        overstretched
        taut but soft
        growing tired   but

        steeped in hope

killed a coconut water and a green juice
before i even rounded the corner onto palmetto
        my body is a temple
                and you
                my darling
                are the only one
                i've ever let
                trash the place

PINEAPPLE

You don't have to do anything
but sit there and I'm salivating
          like I've smelled fresh-cut pineapple

Your body lean as sugar cane
and sweeter
                    I'd like to cut you open
                    suck the tropical marrow

until my tongue stings
until my lips shrivel   then put the rest of you

in the fridge draped in cling wrap
          cause I know I'll want those leftovers

in the middle of the night
when I wake & look all around & settle back to the pillow
& think oh god oh god has this

                    has this all been some
                              delicious some delicious dream?

SERPENT

You're within striking
Dissstance
I see your neck
Pulsing
I want to sink
Softly

Come hither
You already know
I'm a biter
Nothing will
Surprise you
Thisss time around

Don't walk away
I'm still venomousss
I need to move this
Poison around
Somehow

Where are my teeth?
I've lossst my teeth
Dreaming of change

INCHES ONLY

It's 4:02am and I'm struck
by my stubbornness again.

I had stayed hot,
unchanging, for too long.
A slight shift of the head
yields a new cold to the pillow,
a relief inches away.

Inches, inches only.
Would we have moved
if we knew it was that easy?

I still love you (the good kind
of stuck and restless), I love you
under unbreathable sheets, I fight
like kicked off covers, I'll sleep
so damn deep once I find
the sweet spot.

Inches, inches only.
Would we have moved?

SECOND CHANCE

I make love to your absence:
touch myself with your phantom fingers,
compliment your invisible presence
(I love you, you're perfect),
tell your imagined cock it feels amazing,
find your mouth in the crease of my hand
and kiss deeply, promise the static I am open,
wanting it all, ready to be good.
We come together.

I do everything right this time
and the only witness is my heart
that gapes open in the first
slow moment after climax
to remind me I am alone,
pulsing singularly,
clutching sheets only,
and speaking to no one
but the dead, dark air.

RACK

when did it end?   i work   my brain   dry

was it before the sleeping bags zipped apart, you turning to the side
to breathe tent fabric?   perhaps well before the summer of
Wedding Hell™ or   maybe before
the Westby weekend   all cold hands & flat beer
     me too drunk to stand & dance at the Rod & Gun then later
in bed trying to sleep off the other self i'd become

was it   could it have been the first time i tried
to fill my body to the brim with *no bad days*   (the way you said you
wanted me to)   & sloshed all over your carpet to complaint?
anytime i smiled close-mouthed to hold in
the bloody clots of ruptured disappointments?   the last time i
tolerated the tepid droplets of notice you   flicked at me
from your periphery?

     please   baby   throw me a bone

the small caverns behind my eyes roll through with weak light
leaf through weak memory

so hard to write   i rack   i'll go dark before i'll know.

THE OLDEST THING

If the universe is curved,
according to the new paper,
it curves gently.
Not a bed sheet but a balloon,
always a falling away in expansion.

Redo all other calculations!
The oldest thing we know may be wrong.

The edges of the paper are curling;
I've dampened them. Grief just falls,
plants where it lands, deflates itself.
If the universe curves gently, why this heavy,
definite thud?

I redo the calculations.
The oldest thing my body knows is wrong.

SPORE

The conditions are unfavorable.

The garden has taken pity on me.

The wind coaxes the pollen along –
        I cover my mouth.

The light sends a feast –
        I dodge the day.

*

The world is full of clumsy hands
        tall sight lines
        careless boots

Come back and tend to me
Come back and tend

*

Spores arise from a shutting down,
A surrender to survival.
When will it feel like living?
When will I lift my head?

*

Come back and tend to me
Come back and tend to me
Come back and tend to me
Come back and tend

I thought I was doing a good thing,
I thought I would bloom from the rot,
But all I am is myself, and older, and empty.

*

To cut my own stem
To cut my own stem
To cut...I am a coward

I KNOW WHAT YESTERDAY WAS

No smoke show
No sound bath
No energy healing

No pizza down the block
Or laughing through tears
Or dancing in your living room

No outpourings of
Cosmic transcendence
Twin flames
The purest unconditional love

Yesterday I drove through a rain similar to my state
To put my aunt in the ground
A sea of black
A year of death
I don't mean to be bleak but that's the way it goes
I am both feeling and unfeeling

Where's that sheepish slump?
That knowing heart?
That holding of my face in your hands?

I wish you'd found me under the waning moon
My hummingbird heart can't take
Another cracking
Each night it splits to shards in the dark
A deafening ache
Dulled by dawn but never gone

I know what yesterday was
Did you remember too?

NEW YEAR'S DAY

I'm afraid I've become predictable
With all this talk of loneliness

A new year is as good a time as any
To pick up a different hobby
But I am a creature of habit

I'll stay in my grief a bit longer until it
Over coffee or while picking up
Yogurt at the grocery
Crawls from the bags under my eyes
Gives me a last pleading look
And slumps away to visit some other
Poor fool

FIRING SQUAD

A room of my peers
telling me what I do and do not deserve.
Do they know I have my headphones on?
I respect you all so – I really do – but I am
not listening. I will not.

After all this time,
I have only memorized one song,
slight of body and sweating in its repetition.
"Say something different," I dare it.

The lights are harsh. I ask for a glass of water.
Everything feels so sickeningly familiar.

Standing in front of the firing squad,
I can't help but shoot back:

> Who among them has stood inside
> the body of his expanse and cried *Echo*?
> They've whooped and hollered in canyons
> of their own, ones I could not possibly map
> if I tried, so why is their first response to
> discount where a soul in love has been?
>
> We've all lapped at the air between sighs.
> All have stagnated in the aftermath of
> sprayed and salted insults.
> All have pleaded with a deaf god for a life back.

Friends, leave me my delusions.
Let me paint his eyes on the backs of my own. Again.

HOW DOES ANYONE SURVIVE?

Don't think about it today...Ready – Set – Wake!
But it scalds the taste buds on the waves of arabica,
dumps out with the cereal prize, arrives
with the mail, mid-afternoon and delayed,
stuck behind some coupon for eggs.

So you get outta Dodge – out of The States, for God's sake –
where you dance in the Midsummer parade and bathe
in the lakes and sweat in the saunas until you're
bleary-eyed but wide awake.

Where the days overlap like pre-teen chatter, no chance
to cocoon into night, and the light sweeps you up,
clothespins you to the sky – the chance to air-dry those
sopping thoughts in the Finnish countryside.

But as you flutter between the birches it
slices down and perches smack in the middle
of your quiet mind and you think:
How does anyone escape? How does anyone survive?

BETWEEN US

It's neither scars nor scabs;
I scratch my head, I question
the perfection of your skin.
Your eyes still hold me
as your arms once did but
you'd give equal devotion,
the same thirsting glance,
to a sidewalk puddle.
What is it, then, that remains?

Is the answer in the silences?
The static? The seconds between
"Read" and response?
Can it sober up my perceived
meaning of the phrase
I need some time to settle,
but let's connect soon
to a clean-living reality?

Is my unwavering hope
to be trusted in deciphering
that terrifying expanse
of wilderness between us
when I begin – again –
to bloom in your direction?
How closed are your petals?
How cold is it still
in your part of the world?

Will I find anything open,
anything sweet, if I venture out?
I ask the earth in earnest and

in terror, drowning out any answer
before it can speak plainly.
I pick at the sky for particles
that will make up a miracle.
I breathe in deep and beg
to be filled with a different song.
I stay indoors. I wait for the sun.

I know it isn't of this world,
isn't solid, liquid, or gas,
though a closer air descends
down to paperweight
my wind whipped heart
when I stand before you,
when I look in a mirror,
when I claw and bite
and resist surrender,
when I am blown to an edge,
when I am exactly where
I am supposed to be,
when I am anywhere,
anywhere at all.

I am thick with it,
whatever this is
between us.

PICK

I'm having trouble knowing what to say.
I've drained my battery re-writing notes,
trying not to beg or apologize.
Directness seems harsh when "Sorry."
is the customary response.

My phone's camera cannot capture
the sunlit web in the corner of the garden –
there are too many strings,
the wind ripple almost imperceptible.

I ask the open morning: "When can a memory rest?"

I sit and pick at shoulder scabs,
routine at this point, a terrible tick
I always say I'll fix.
"Sorry."
I always bleed, redden, scar over.
"Sorry."
I always do it again.

LIKE HONEY BEES

What if I told you
you'd been going about it
all wrong?
Alone, that is.

Would you believe me
if I said that I'd washed
my body clean of the stick
and the muck and this time
I was sure of it?

I will sting you again.
We will sting each other again.
It is what happens
in any unfurling and refolding.

But unlike the yellow jacket,
that repeat offender,
I will not continue to attack.
As slow and as sorry as a honey bee,
I will remove my weapon
and be done with it.

I offer this life to you,
buzzing in cupped hands.
Will you let the hum catch
in your throat once more?

IF THE DICE HAD BEEN BELLS

If the dice had been bells when I rolled them,
          my loss would've a silvery echo,
          my disappointment a tinny grin.

Hope isn't weighted in favor of fate –
          it jangles even, lands random.

          A card table of ash and wobbling rings
          from drinks picked up, ice sucked –

          All eyes and minds shooting forward
          toward my failure –

          Where's the pretty girl,
          blotted lip and quiet breath,
          to blow into my knuckles for luck?

          "Yes, quiet now...I'd like to hear them."

If the dice had been bells when I rolled them,
          if they'd been bells,
          it would've been the last sweet din I let in.

KUUSI PALAA

"It's all in the context," Saku told me,
his fifth beer in his right hand,
his second cigarette in his left.
"In Finnish, we have
thousands of ways
to say the same thing."

Six pieces
Six returns
The moon is returning
"Kuusi Palaa"

And you can forget about Love,
about throwing it around.
Rakastan reserved only
for the deepest declaration,
for something my English
cannot touch.

Were I a native speaker,
were you,
maybe then we could've trusted
those sacred transactions.

Maybe then we could've known
in what context to quit.

Maybe then a relationship
in thousands of pieces
could make thousands of returns.

The moon comes back to hang high,
Rakastan to hang on our lips.

LOVE: INFINITE / VISIBILITY: POOR

Edges peeling,
            my smile breaking
            its own record,
flecks of the end
dusting my lashes,
            Gillian Welch on the speakers.

            A fight aftertaste,
                        but he's brewing us
                        a fragrant tea;
            Scrabble has been set.

                        I shimmer in holograph
                                    How He Wants Me: Barely There

                                                            Love: Infinite

Visibility: Poor

Sharp sun spires
suspend his eyes in time,
memory membranes pierced.

It's been two years,
god damn it,
and these bright shards
won't relent.

Edges peel,
reveal more
edges to peel.
My heart still breaking;
a new record.

I shimmer among the refracted past
His Aftertaste: Barely There

LIGHTER NOW

THE JUMPER

A suit with little room for much else
Except a pooling of fear
At the throat perhaps,
Where the zipper starts.

I search the lineup for his red and white,
His shape merely a suggestion
From the height he climbs to.
A miniature carrying two chopsticks –
I will never know the true weight of those utensils,
But I have felt the true weight of the jumper.

He appears on the inrun in a blink.
He breathes in long and slow,
The same ice caught in my lungs.
A flicker, and he is sliding.
Another, and he's gone.

Next time we meet he is airborne,
A stamp on the sky.
Gravity would tell us he's floating down
But I don't trust it – he seems so
Beautifully suspended, an ornament
Hung on some weighty, invisible hook.

But eventually he does touch down,
An easy glide into the landing;
Past the crowds, past me,
Past all possible darkness.

Since then, the snows have
Sloughed off the slopes and
He and I have gone into

A different kind of sliding.
On my best days I wish him well,
I loosen my grip,
Something melts.

I miss the jumper.
I think of him every day.
No longer mine,
I charge the sky with his care
And remind myself, ritual-like,
As if carving deep grooves for skis,
That I want to love like he jumps
And to live like he lands.

NEW HEIGHTS

A rose reaches beyond fencing –
folds unseen from the ground.
An inner mapping: hidden.
An interior life: guessed.

A rose speaks of summer's peaking end –
petals intact but no longer
pulsing with June's promise
of warm and fickle rain.

A rose as a gift for sorrows –
fragrant, bundled condolences
wake a momentary glitter in the eye
but cannot resurrect the hope.

A rose runs a fool's errand –
you see: he never had a scent
for fragility and grace;
spare the bend to eye level.

A rose searches beyond fencing –
uncurls pastel palms to honeyed light,
evades pruning shears,
safe in its singular atmosphere,
gracious in its patience for August's collapse,
knowing that this year
it soared to new heights.

THE WILDFLOWER

How serendipitous
to have noticed the wildflower
on your journey,
that you had noticed each other.

But what a shame
it is now protected,
endangered,
and cannot be picked,
not even by the kindest hand.

Or perhaps,
just maybe,
to admire it while
it is still rooted,
without laying claim,
without plucking it up
to slowly wilt under
the sun on the windowsill
or in the warmth of your palm,
is the greatest blessing,
the most reverent kind of care.

BLOOD-REMEMBERING

I have not fallen out of love
(my hooks too deep for that behavior) –
No, I have not fallen out.

It goes like this:
I shed the blistered skin.
I stuff the hollowed heart.
I let the days water my eyes
from puckered to plump until

I am perched anew,
bobbing at the edge,
the cusp before the plunge.
Molted clean, a chest
of feathers, as light
as the moment before
I was first struck down
by it all.

Though there still will sit
a sting of something, curled
just below the chin, waiting
to be salved, recognized,
remembered as part of blood, of skin,
of cells energized by that first
flicker of light in a dark place that,
it turns out, has been brilliantly painted
with the breadth of the color spectrum,
has been perfectly preserved, and has been
waiting for me, just as I am, to settle back in.

ONE MORNING

One morning you will wake
having cut through a darkness
so pure in its black
you won't recognize the day.
But some ancient rhythm within
will remember the warmth
of sun on skin and
you will kiss the ground
though it be wet and clodded
and rise with soft grain on your lips
tasting the hidden sweetness
in the metaled loam.
People will stare at you
thinking you mad.
You will stare at them
like you've never been hurt before.

A LETTER TO THE ONE I'M WAITING FOR

To Whom It Will Concern:

Do you ache for the quiver in my step
as I approach on soft moss?

Oh, and hello *(forgive me, introductions escape me*
when I teeter on the brink of bright flashes).

I'll begin again:
How are you?
Who are you?
Do you anticipate my arrival,
as I do yours?

I'm afraid I've not had much luck:
Swimming upstream, an unforgiving river,
dead fish slopping down the falls as I
shoulder out of the muck.
Put another way: Love has come (and gone)
like a pinprick. It shocks/stings/smarts
the finger pad, then evaporates in the wake
of the cosmic accident, the digit
retaining the throb, blood gathering
where surface air meets sebaceous gland.

But then there's You:
the end to my flopping about,
my sucking of index fingers.

I approach on soft moss.
Do you ache?

I try to remain optimistic
with my "*Will* Concern,"
but the kernel of the absolute
lies in its non-existence,
in its very un-American un-guarantee.
Perhaps there is no recipient.
Perhaps Recipient is Writer.
Perhaps I am "going it alone."

But I'd to think there is a "You,"
a hearth for my heart.
It keeps me light, keeps me
going outside, keeps me
filling my cup so I can
runneth it over.

My tread is lithe, the moss plush.
Do you ache for the quiver in my step?

Sincerely Yours,

The One You're Waiting For

ACKNOWLEDGEMENTS

I'd like to thank *Hobart Journal* for the publication of Cycle and Pineapple in November of 2019 and *Else Journal* for the publication of The Walk Home in May of 2020.

Thanks as well to the generous eyes and ears of my fellow poets, friends, and sisters in heartbreak, who read and listened to these poems throughout their evolution.

A special shout out to Jennifer Hart for her editing prowess and for teaching me how to (gently) kill my darlings.

+

"If the universe is curved, according to the new paper, it curves gently" is a quote from *The Universe Might Be a Giant Loop*, a Live Science article by Rafi Letzer.

"If the dice had been bells when I rolled them" is a line borrowed from *Regret*, a poem by Kelly Turwilliger.

+

This collection is for Cooper.

"I want you to know, if you ever read this...I would rather have had you by my side than any one of these words."
- Maggie Nelson

+

For those who can find solace in these pages, this is for you too. I wish you lightness.

Finally: this is for myself, and for what I hope to find.

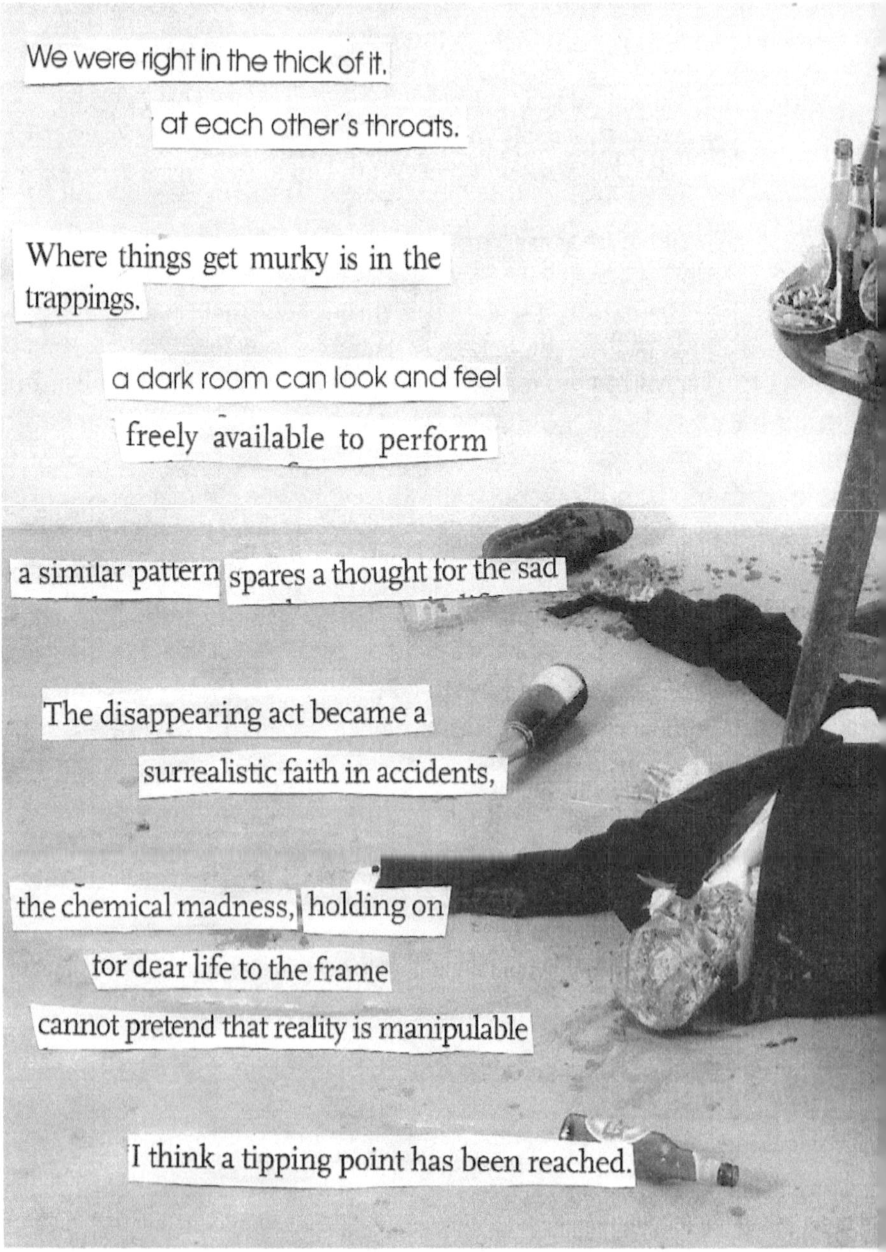

We were right in the thick of it.
at each other's throats.

Where things get murky is in the
trappings.
a dark room can look and feel
freely available to perform

a similar pattern spares a thought for the sad

The disappearing act became a
surrealistic faith in accidents,

the chemical madness, holding on
for dear life to the frame
cannot pretend that reality is manipulable

I think a tipping point has been reached.

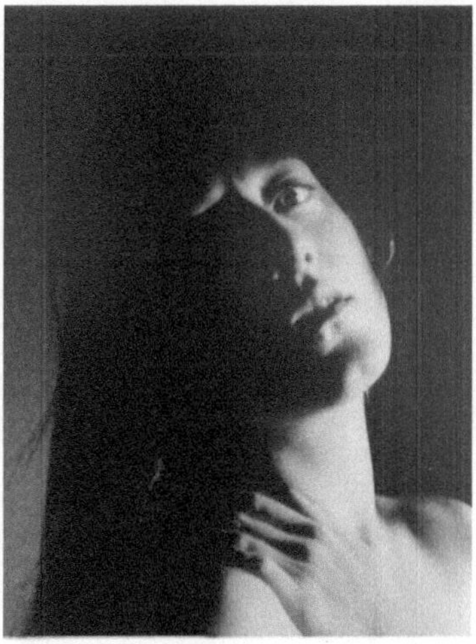

Hannah Donovan is a poet, photographer, and visual artist from Northern California. Her work has been featured in *Hobart, The Accouont, Else Journal, Hill Lily Magazine, The Artist Essentials*, the Black Box Gallery (Portland, OR), New System Exhibitions (Portland, ME), and Maine College of Art (Portland, ME). She has been a finalist for Brooklyn Poet's "Poem of the Year" competition and an artist-in-residence at the Arteles Creative Center in Finland. Other publications include *Ice Chips* (Ethel Micro-Press), *deadend* (palindrome press), and *Dim Dimmer Dark* (palindrome press). She lives in Los Angeles.

www.hannahdonovanart.com

www.ingramcontent.com/pod-product-compliance
Lightning Source LLC
Chambersburg PA
CBHW022203160726
48282CB00024B/306
* 9 7 8 8 1 1 9 6 5 4 0 7 9 *